American Democracy in Action

The Constitution: The Responsibilities and Powers of the U.S. Government

Cathleen Small

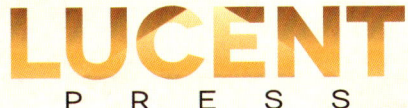

LUCENT PRESS

Published in 2019 by
Lucent Press, an Imprint of Greenhaven Publishing, LLC
353 3rd Avenue
Suite 255
New York, NY 10010

Produced for Lucent by Calcium Creative Ltd
Designers: Clare Webber and Simon Borrough
Picture researcher: Rachel Blount
Editors: Sarah Eason and Jennifer Sanderson

Picture credits: Cover: Shutterstock: Pamela Au (top), Welcomia (bottom).
Inside: Shutterstock: Blend Images: p. 32; Charles Brutlag: p. 7; Orhan Cam: p. 15; Rob
Crandall: p. 38; Designer491: p. 42; Everett Historical: pp. 10–11, 20, 22, 30; Festa: p. 17;
Michaella Hughes: p. 28; Andrea Izzotti: p. 12; Gina Jacobs: p. 36; Georgios Kollidas: p. 13;
Mark Reinstein: p. 39; ShutterOK: p. 35; Sirtravelalot: p. 41; Joseph Sohm: pp. 5, 44–45;
Tooykrub: p. 26; Wikimedia Commons: Brendanghs: p. 23; Henry P. Moore: p. 18; Hans
Peters/Anefo: p. 24; John Trumbull: p. 9; John Vanderlyn (1775–1852): p. 6.

Cataloging-in-Publication Data

Names: Small, Cathleen.
Title: The Constitution: the responsibilities and powers of the U.S. government / Cathleen
Small.
Description: New York : Lucent Press, 2019. | Series: American democracy in action |
Includes glossary and index.
Identifiers: ISBN 9781534564084 (pbk.) | ISBN 9781534564060 (library bound)
Subjects: LCSH: United States. Constitution--Juvenile literature. | Constitutional history--
United States--Juvenile literature.
Classification: LCC E303.S63 2019 | DDC 342.7302'9--dc23

Printed in the United States of America

CPSIA compliance information: Batch #BS18KL: For further information,
contact Greenhaven Publishing, LLC, New York, New York, at 1-844-317-7404.

Please visit our website, www.greenhavenpublishing.com.
For a free color catalog of all our high-quality books,
call toll free 1-844-317-7404 or fax 1-844-317-7405.

Contents

CHAPTER 1

Understanding the Constitution

The United States Constitution is considered the law of the land. It is the document on which the nation's government structure is based, and it is the document the judicial system looks to when deciding complicated legal cases. However, the Constitution was written more than 200 years ago, when the nation was in its infancy. Somehow, though, it has stood the test of time.

A constitution is a collection of principles or **precedents** by which a state or other organization is governed. Any sort of organization or territory can have a constitution. The U.S. Constitution, however, is unique in that it governs an entire nation of more than 321 million people. Somehow, it manages to do so quite effectively, despite being a relatively short document.

The Preamble

The purpose of the Constitution is summed up in its preamble, which states, "We the People of the United States, in Order to form a more perfect Union, establish Justice, insure domestic Tranquility, provide for the common defence, promote the general Welfare, and secure the Blessings of Liberty to ourselves and our Posterity, do ordain and establish this Constitution for the United States of America."

These are lot of goals for one document. Establishing justice alone is a big undertaking. So is ensuring domestic tranquility, or peace.

Some people find that hard to do in their own homes, much less for a whole nation. Yet the **Framers of the Constitution** were confident that they could achieve those goals and more—they could also promote citizens' general welfare and ensure liberty for all.

How It Works

The Framers made the Constitution work by balancing specifics with open language. They set forth very definite rules about things such as presidential terms, terms for members of Congress, eligibility requirements for the president and members of Congress, how elections would occur, how the government power would be structured, and what the rights and responsibilities of states would be in relation to the federal government.

However, the Framers of the Constitution also left the language open in many instances because they recognized that the state of the nation in the late 1700s was not necessarily going to be the same in the future. For example, even though slavery was an institution in the late 1700s, it is never specifically mentioned in the original Constitution. It is implied, such as in Article I, Section 2, where "other Persons" are said to count as three-fifths of a "free Person." It is also implied in Article IV, Section 2, which discusses "Person[s] held to Service or Labour." However, it is not explicitly stated—at least in part because slavery was already a controversial topic, and the Framers knew it was not necessarily going to be around forever.

The Statue of Liberty and the Constitution are two icons symbolizing the United States of America.

Perfecting an Imperfect Document

Although the original Constitution was a largely effective document, it was not perfect. Specifically, its loose language in some areas left a great deal of power in the hands of the federal government, which was concerning to some states and citizens. Congress argued that the Constitution could not simply be rewritten, so James Madison addressed concerns by writing a series of amendments. Madison wrote the first 10 amendments, and they are collectively known as the Bill of Rights. They further set out what powers are to be held by states and what the federal government's powers are.

Since then, changes to the Constitution have been made in the form of amendments. Today, there are 27 amendments to the Constitution.

The Law of the Land

As the law of the land, the Constitution touches every part of government in the United States. To understand its reach, it helps to understand the background of United States before the Constitution went into effect, and how the Constitution is used in relation to each branch of government, especially the judicial branch. You will then have a good idea of the importance of this relatively short document.

James Madison was one of the Framers of the Constitution. He wrote the Bill of Rights.

CONSTITUTIONS IN OTHER NATIONS

The United States is not unique in having a constitution that governs the nation. In fact, many nations do. The United States Constitution is, however, the oldest codified constitution.

A codified constitution is one in which the laws or rules are formally arranged and collected, and recognized as absolute law. Codified law is different from common law, which is law developed by judges and courts based on precedent. So, for example, a judge might consider common law when deciding a case—looking to past legal decisions that support a decision in the case at hand. However, the judge would also consider the codified law put forth in the Constitution. Common law can be more easily challenged and changed, especially if constitutional law (which is naturally codified) suggests that common law may not be fair. Codified law is much more difficult to challenge or change.

The Bill of Rights contains the first 10 amendments to the Constitution.

While the United States has the oldest codified constitution, one of the newest codified constitutions belongs to the country of Thailand. There are also uncodified constitutions, where not all of the constitutional elements are formally written into law. Among the nations that have uncodified constitutions are Canada, New Zealand, and the United Kingdom.

CHAPTER 2

Before the Constitution

The U.S. Constitution was signed on September 17, 1787, at the Constitutional Convention. It was **ratified** by 11 of the original 13 states in 1788, and the 2 remaining states (North Carolina and Rhode Island) ratified it in 1790. The signing and ratification of the Constitution was not the beginning of the United States. The United States had existed as an independent nation from 1776. The Declaration of Independence was drafted and signed in 1776.

The Declaration of Independence

When colonists and Pilgrims came to America to settle, the land was still largely under British rule. Portions of the land were also under French, Dutch, and Spanish rule. The United States as it is known today did not exist. Tensions were high, and by the 1760s, those tensions began to boil over. Protests, boycotts, and other resistance efforts began to spring up. In April 1775, the resistance turned into open combat and brought about the beginning of the Revolutionary War.

The Continental Congress, which had been formed by representatives from the 13 colonies, issued the official Declaration of Independence on July 4, 1776—just 2 days after the congress voted for independence. The 13 colonies were already at war with Great Britain, but the Declaration of Independence made a formal announcement. From that point forward, the 13 colonies would be **sovereign states**, collectively gathered into a new nation called the United States of America. They would be free from British rule.

The Declaration of Independence was written by Thomas Jefferson, and edited by John Adams and Benjamin Franklin. Before ratifying the document, Congress made a few changes. By early August 1776, Congress had signed it.

The Declaration of Independence was not a law of the land like the Constitution is. Rather, it was a document designed to declare independence, and to argue and explain why it should be granted. It listed the failings of England's King George III in the eyes of the colonists. It also called on natural and legal rights as a reason why independence should be granted. Perhaps the most famous line of the document declares, "We hold these truths to be self-evident, that all men are created equal, that they are endowed by their Creator with certain unalienable Rights, that among these are Life, Liberty, and the pursuit of Happiness." Unalienable means those rights cannot be taken away or denied.

So while the Declaration of Independence did not necessarily set forth laws for the new nation, it did set forth the overall goals for the nation and the rights of its citizens. As such, it is an important document in the history of the United States.

This artist's representation shows the signing of the Declaration of Independence.

The Articles of Confederation

Shortly after the Declaration of Independence was issued, the Second Continental Congress began working on the Articles of Confederation, which would serve as the first constitution for the new nation. It took more than a year for the Second Continental Congress to finalize a draft that would be sent to the states for ratification in November 1777. It took nearly four more years for the Articles of Confederation to be ratified by all 13 states and enforced. However, the ratification of the Articles was more of a formality than anything—the states were already operating in the manner described in the Articles, as was the central government (what later became the federal government).

The Articles of Confederation granted most power to the individual states. The central government was actually fairly weak and did not have much power over the day-to-day operations of the states. It quickly became apparent that this approach was problematic. The citizens of the United States were trying to establish a new nation, but that new nation would only hold together if there were some unifying force holding it together.

The Continental Congress, which by then was going by the name of the Confederation Congress, heard requests from citizens for changes to the Articles of Confederation. The Congress recognized the inherent weakness in the government and the power structure set up in the Articles. As a result, they set a Constitutional Convention to take place in Philadelphia, Pennsylvania, in May 1787. There, discussion would begin about a new constitution to define the government and power of the land.

The debate about the power structure set up in the Articles of Confederation is mirrored in some ways today. Many people today feel that the federal government has too much power, and that power should be handed over to state governments. They feel this will give more **autonomy** to individual states, and will allow more freedoms, depending on state governments. However, those who prefer the federal government to hold the majority of power feel that handing power over to the individual states could create problems of inequality. For example, citizens' rights in one state would not be the same in another state. What do you think? In terms of citizens' rights, do you think a federal government with a uniform policy is better, or do you think states should make their own decisions? Why or why not?

Future president George Washington presided over the Constitutional Convention in Philadelphia. The Convention is one of the most significant events in the history of the United States because the Constitution was written there.

The Constitutional Convention

The Constitutional Convention convened in Philadelphia on May 25, 1787. It was presided over by George Washington, who would later become the first president of the United States. Originally, the aim was to revise the Articles of Confederation to address the weaknesses in it. Specifically, they wanted to revise the language that allowed the central government to be a weak force, with the bulk of power being given to the states.

However, some members of the Constitutional Convention argued that a wiser move would be to start from scratch and create an entirely new document and government structure. James Madison and Alexander Hamilton were both in favor of this plan for creating an entirely new government.

While waiting for all of the delegates to assemble in Philadelphia so a **quorum** could be established, James Madison drafted the Virginia Plan, which inspired much of the Constitution. Among other things, the Virginia Plan set forth the idea of a **bicameral** Congress. The New Jersey Plan presented by William Paterson argued that a **unicameral** Congress was more appropriate. The delegates eventually decided to use the elements of the Virginia Plan, and a bicameral Congress was established.

Independence Hall is where both the Declaration of Independence and the Constitution were adopted.

MEMBERS OF THE CONSTITUTIONAL CONVENTION

Altogether, 55 men attended the Constitutional Convention as delegates from 12 of the 13 states: Rhode Island did not send a delegate. More than half had fought in or held commanding positions in the Revolutionary War. More than half were trained lawyers, though not all had practiced. Nearly half owned slaves. Most had served in state or colonial government, and most had been members of the Confederation Congress. Two delegates, Roger Sherman and Robert Morris, signed the Declaration of Independence, the Articles of Confederation, and the Constitution.

George Washington presided over the Convention, but many other noteworthy men served on it, too, including Benjamin Franklin and James Madison. Many people assume John Hancock's famous signature is on the Constitution, but it is not—Hancock was not part of the Convention. Nor were several other notable figures in history, such as Thomas Jefferson, John Adams, and Patrick Henry.

In total, 16 of the delegates did not sign the final draft of the Constitution. Yet, it still passed and was adopted as the law of the land.

George Washington may be the most famous face of the Constitutional Convention.

Separation of Powers

The members of the Convention determined that for the United States to run effectively and be a strong nation, there needed to be a **separation of powers** and a system of **checks and balances**. This is similar to the British government system under which they had previously lived. Although Great Britain has long had a monarch (a king or queen), the monarch actually does not hold a lot of power. The monarch is more of a figurehead for the nation—a symbol of unity and a figure to whom the public can look toward as a sign of their nation. Much more of the power in the British government lies with Parliament. However, the monarch and Parliament work together to promote the best interests of the nation. In the United States, there are three branches of government to promote the best interests of the nation.

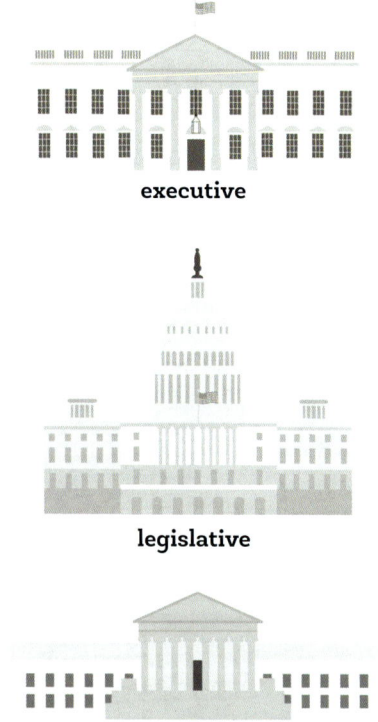

executive

legislative

judicial

The executive branch of government is the president of the United States and a number of people who work beneath the president. The legislative branch is made up of the two chambers of Congress—the Senate and the House of Representatives. This branch creates the laws under which the nation is run. The judicial branch is made up of the Supreme Court and federal courts, all of which interpret and uphold the Constitution and the laws made under it. These three branches of government are each given different duties and powers.

The United States' separation of powers is achieved by dividing power among the three branches of government: the executive, legislative, and judicial branches.

This helps create the system of checks and balances that ensures that no single branch or person is given too much power in governing the United States. All three branches work together—particularly the executive and legislative branches. The judicial branch then carries out—or overturns—the laws set forth by the legislative branch and signed off by the executive branch.

The overall government structure and power was a fairly agreeable point during the Constitutional Convention. However, the details of what this would look like were the source of much debate at the Convention. For example, members of the Convention argued over the specific eligibility details for the president, how long a president could serve, how citizens would be represented (for example, would slaves be counted as people?), how members of the Senate would be elected, and so on. These details would require much debate and discussion among the delegates at the convention.

Congress meets at the United States Capitol in Washington, D.C.

CHAPTER 3

Drafting the Constitution

Drafting the Constitution was a long, arduous process at the Constitutional Convention. For the better part of 4 months, the 55 delegates debated many points before setting them down in the document that would become the law of the land for the United States. While many consider James Madison to be the author of the Constitution, in reality, there were 55 contributing authors. James Madison mainly took notes and wrote everything down.

Getting Started

The 55 delegates who gathered in Philadelphia were there for one common purpose: the Articles of Confederation were not sufficient as a governing document for the new nation. Citizens needed a new constitution that would set forth the overall governing principles and laws for the United States.

The preamble to the Constitution explains the delegates' goal: "We the People of the United States, in Order to form a more perfect Union, establish Justice, insure domestic Tranquility, provide for the common defence, promote the general Welfare, and secure the Blessings of Liberty to ourselves and our Posterity, do ordain and establish this Constitution for the United States of America."

The four words that really sum up the goal of the Constitution are "a more perfect Union." The United States was functioning before the Constitution, but imperfectly. Perfection is an impossible goal, but "a more perfect Union" could be reached.

It took roughly four months to debate and draft the U.S. Constitution.

They wanted something that would function much more close to perfectly. It was needed, so the delegates got to work.

While the document was composed by the delegates, the opening phrase "We the People" indicates that the Constitution was designed to uphold the rights of all U.S. citizens. The delegates were just that: delegates of the body of citizens that made up the United States.

The Original Constitution

The original Constitution, before the Bill of Rights and other amendments were added, consisted of seven articles. The first three articles set out the separation of powers into an executive, a legislative, and a judicial branch. The next three articles outlined **federalism** and how states would function under the federal government. The final article described the ratification process.

Although the Constitutional Convention began on May 14, 1787, a quorum was not achieved until May 25, 1787. In those first 11 days, James Madison from Virginia worked on the Virginia Plan, which later became a model for the Constitution. The Virginia Plan was considered by a **Committee of the Whole** beginning on May 31, 1787. Shortly thereafter, the New Jersey Plan was also considered as an option.

The Connecticut Compromise

One big difference between the Virginia Plan and the New Jersey Plan was that the Virginia Plan suggested a bicameral Congress, while the New Jersey Plan suggested a unicameral Congress. The plans also affected how states were represented in Congress. The delegates of the Constitutional Convention were concerned about the possibility of certain states achieving more representation in Congress than others. So, on July 2, 1787, a Committee of Eleven, created with one delegate from each state represented, met to work out the issue of representation in Congress.

Over a period of two weeks, the Committee of Eleven debated the issue, then wrote a report known as the Connecticut Compromise. The Connecticut Compromise kept the bicameral structure of Congress and proposed two different types of representation.

When the Constitution was drafted, slaves were still considered to be property in the southern states.

In the Senate, they proposed that each state would have two representatives, elected by the state's legislators. A later amendment changed the policy so that senators would be elected directly by citizens in a **popular vote**. They also proposed that each state would be represented in the House of Representatives by a number of representatives directly proportional to the population of the state. In other words, states with a higher population would have more representatives. The House system is still in place today, with heavily populated states such as California and New York having many representatives, and less-populated states such as Wyoming and Alaska having few.

The Three-Fifths Compromise

Another question during the Constitutional Convention was how people would be counted as citizens. The number of citizens in a state determined how much representation that state would have in the House of Representatives, so it was extremely important that the Framers of the Constitution set out how citizenship would be counted.

The issue was mostly about slaves. At the time, slaves were considered property, not people. Slaveholding was particularly common in the South at that time. So it was in Southerners' best interests for slaves to be counted as people, because it would boost the population numbers in the South, resulting in greater representation in Congress. Since the South wanted to see slaveholding, among other things, supported in Congress, they wanted as much representation as possible. Slaves also were not allowed to vote, which meant that Southerners would get the best of both worlds—greater representation in Congress, but without the danger of slaves voting against the policies the Southerners wanted to see supported.

It was cruelly ironic that Southerners saw slaves as property, but wanted them counted as people. People who were against slavery (mostly Northerners) did not want slaves counted as people, because they did not want slaveholding states to have more power in Congress.

The delegates enacted the Three-Fifths Compromise and wrote the following language into the Constitution: "Representatives and direct Taxes shall be apportioned among the several States which may be included within this Union, according to their respective Numbers, which shall be determined by adding to the whole Number of free Persons, including those bound to Service for a Term of Years, and excluding Indians not taxed, three fifths of all other Persons." So, for purposes of taxation and representation, each slave counted as three-fifths of a person.

The Three-Fifths Compromise did not grant slaves any political representation. It only strengthened the political power of slaveholders.

The phrase "those bound to Service for a Term of Years" is thought to refer to **indentured servants**, who were counted as people for the purposes of taxation and representation. Indentured servants were immigrants who entered brutal contracts in order to come to the United States. Indentured servants were bound to serve only for an agreed-upon length of time (usually, several years), while they worked to "pay off" their passage to the United States. After the indentured servant fulfilled the terms of their contract, they would eventually be granted citizenship and given their freedom.

SLAVERY IN THE CONSTITUTION

Slavery was a huge issue during the drafting of the Constitution, but the original Constitution never mentions the words "slave" or "slavery." The Framers of the Constitution were aware that slavery was a controversial topic, and they wanted the Constitution to stand the test of time. Would slavery still be legal in the future United States? They could not be sure, so they drafted the Constitution in such a way that slavery was addressed but not specifically mentioned.

The first way in which they did so was with the Three-Fifths clause, found in Article I, Section 2. The second general mention of the concept of slavery came in Article I, Section 9, which reads, "The Migration and Importation of such Persons as any of the States now existing shall think proper to admit, shall not be prohibited by the Congress prior to the Year one thousand eight hundred and eight, but a Tax or duty may be imposed on such Importation, not exceeding ten dollars for each Person." In other words, current states in the United States would be permitted to choose whether to allow importation of slaves at least until 1808, but Congress could put a tax on the imported slaves.

Further on, in Article IV, Section 2, the fugitive-slave clause appears: "No Person held to Service or Labour in one State, under the Laws thereof, escaping into another, shall, in Consequence of any Law or Regulation therein, be discharged from such Service or Labour, but shall be delivered up on Claim of the Party to whom Service or Labour may be due." This meant that if a slave escaped to a free state, under the Constitution, they would be returned to the slave owner.

The Committees

Near the end of July, the Convention determined that it had discussed and agreed on most of its differences, so it assembled a Committee of Detail consisting of five delegates from South Carolina, Virginia, Massachusetts, Connecticut, and Pennsylvania. These delegates were tasked with drafting a constitution that incorporated all the decisions and compromises that had been made by the Convention up to that point. On August 6, 1787, the Committee of Detail presented its draft, which had 23 articles and a preamble.

Hamilton was a member of the Committee of Style and Arrangement. He was the first Secretary of the Treasury and wrote economic policies in the Washington administration.

The Convention then reviewed the draft piece by piece, line by line, discussing every detail and making further changes and compromises. This tedious process took more than a month. On September 8, 1787, a new committee was formed called the Committee of Style and Arrangement. This committee consisted of five members—among them Alexander Hamilton and James Madison.

The Committee of Style and Arrangement reworked and clarified the 23 articles into a final draft of the Constitution, containing a preamble and 7 articles.

The final version was not an overall success with the delegates at the Convention, though. Some felt too many compromises had been made. Three delegates refused to sign the Constitution, and others left before the ceremony. Still, there were enough supporters from the 12 states represented to deem that the signing of the Constitution was an overall success.

This is a copy of the second draft of the Constitution, complete with notes in the margin.

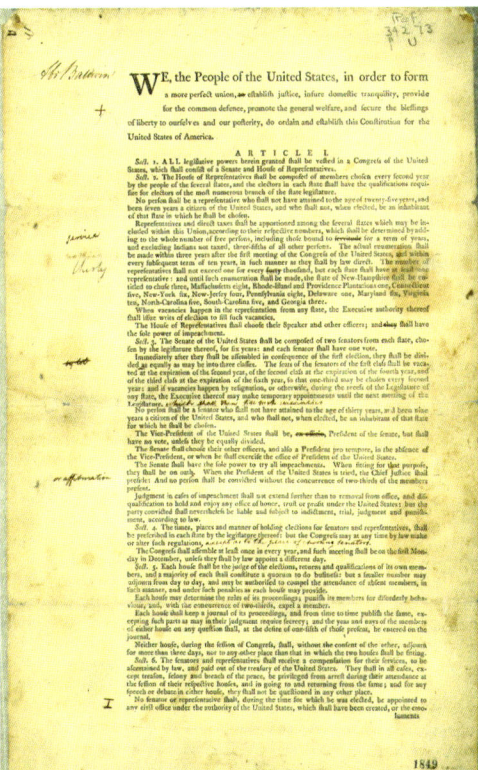

Adopting the Constitution

After the Constitution was signed, it had to be ratified by each of the 13 states. By 1788, 11 states had ratified it, and the remaining 2 states (North Carolina and Rhode Island) did so by 1790. The Constitution had to be ratified only by two-thirds of the states (nine at that time) to go into effect, so it went into effect on March 4, 1789. This is the same day the Congress of the Confederation was dissolved, and the same day the first session of the current Congress of the United States began. The first president, George Washington, took office in May 1789.

CHAPTER 4

The Amendments

The Constitution itself is not very long—just a preamble and seven articles. It was soon expanded when the Bill of Rights, written by James Madison, was added in 1791. The Bill of Rights was a response to citizens and states that wanted specific limitations put on federal power.

If the Titles of Nobility Amendment had been passed, Princess Grace of Monaco would have had to give up her U.S. citizenship.

The Bill of Rights

Originally, Madison wanted to amend the Constitution to address the issues covered in the Bill of Rights. However, his fellow members of Congress in the House of Representatives argued that Congress did not have the right to change the wording of the Constitution. They finally settled on adding the Bill of Rights as the first 10 amendments instead.

Originally, the Bill of Rights was to contain 17 amendments. The House of Representatives passed all 17 amendments, but the Senate only approved 12. Then, the states ratified 10 of those 12 amendments. So, the Bill of Rights contains the first 10 amendments to the Constitution. The Bill of Rights does not contain all the amendments to the Constitution, though. Over the years, a total of 27 amendments have been added to the United States Constitution.

PENDING OR CLOSED AMENDMENTS

While 27 amendments have been added to the Constitution, a total of 33 have been proposed. The six that have not been ratified include four that are pending (awaiting a decision), and two that are closed. The six unratified amendments are:

- The Congressional Apportionment Amendments, which has been pending since 1789 and proposes to regulate the size of state congressional districts.

- The Titles of Nobility Amendment, which has been pending since 1810, would remove citizenship status from any U.S. citizen who accepts a title of nobility from a foreign country.

- The Corwin Amendment, which has been pending since 1861 and would make slavery immune to **abolition** by Congress. Given that Congress abolished slavery in the Thirteenth Amendment, this amendment is meaningless.

- The Child Labor Amendment, which has been pending since 1924 and would let the federal government limit, regulate, and prohibit child labor. Child labor laws do exist, so this amendment is essentially not important now.

- The Equal Rights Amendment, which failed in 1982, is closed. It would have prohibited federal and state governments from depriving people of equal rights based on their gender. The Equal Protection Clause in the Fourteenth Amendment mostly covers this issue.

- The District of Columbia Voting Rights Amendment, which failed in 1985 and is closed. This would have treated Washington, D.C., as a state (rather than as a federal district), giving it equal representation in Congress and the **electoral college**. Washington, D.C., was granted electoral votes as part of the Twenty-Third Amendment, but that amendment did not address the issue of equal representation in Congress.

First Amendment

The First Amendment, was ratified in 1791. It covers a number of issues, including freedom of religion, freedom of speech, freedom of the press, and the right to peacefully assemble. Given that the United States bills itself as the "home of the free," this amendment is incredibly important.

Second Amendment

The Second Amendment, ratified in 1791, protects the rights of citizens to bear arms, or own guns. This amendment is a frequent source of debate between the Democratic and Republican parties. While there are exceptions in any party, in general, Republicans are in favor of the Second Amendment and are fiercely protective of private citizens' right to keep guns. Many Democrats, on the other hand, feel that gun restrictions should be tighter and more restrictive. They point to issues of gun violence in cities and mass shootings in schools and public places, which have become far more common in recent years, as reasons for why gun rights should be more limited than they are. It is certainly possible for these parties to reach a compromise on gun ownership. However, the topic of gun control is often very emotional on both sides.

The Second Amendment may be the most debated of the amendments in the Bill of Rights. This sculpture called Non-Violence can be seen at the United Nations Headquarters in Manhattan, New York City.

Gun control was a central issue in the 2016 presidential election. Supporters of the Second Amendment worried that if Hillary Clinton were elected president, she and Congress would work toward stricter gun laws. People who support gun regulation worried that if Donald Trump were elected, the United States would not see any improvement in decreasing gun violence.

Third Amendment

The Third Amendment, ratified in 1791, prevents soldiers from lodging in private homes without the homeowner's consent during peacetime. Previously, armies could force homeowners to give them lodging.

Fourth Amendment

Ratified in 1791, the Fourth Amendment limits the right of law enforcement in terms of search and seizure. It establishes that, before searching a person's home, law enforcement must have a search warrant issued by a judge and based on probable cause, or reasonable suspicion.

Fifth Amendment

The Fifth Amendment was ratified in 1791. It protects citizens' rights to **due process**. It also prohibits **double jeopardy** and **self-incrimination**, and it establishes that a person cannot be held for a crime without grand jury **indictment**.

Sixth Amendment

The Sixth Amendment was also ratified in 1791. It guarantees citizens the right to trial by a jury of their peers, carried out in a fair and speedy manner. It also establishes that accused criminals be notified about their accusations, be given a chance to confront their accuser in a court of law, and be given the chance to retain legal counsel and obtain witnesses for a trial.

Seventh Amendment

The Seventh Amendment, ratified in 1791, guarantees the right to a jury trial for certain civil offenses.

Eighth Amendment

The Eighth Amendment, prohibits cruel and unusual punishment. It was ratified in 1791. This was an important amendment, since punishments in the early days of history could be very brutal, or violent. This amendment also establishes that any fines issued for a crime must not be extreme.

The Eighth Amendment protects U.S. citizens from cruel and unusual punishment, such as this medieval dunking cage used during witch trials.

Ninth Amendment

The Ninth Amendment rather vaguely protects citizens' rights that are not spelled out in the Constitution. It was ratified in 1791.

Tenth Amendment

The Tenth Amendment, ratified in 1791, grants the federal government only powers given to it by the states or the people through the Constitution. Any powers not given to the federal government belongs to states and/or citizens.

Eleventh Amendment

The Eleventh Amendment, ratified in 1795, protects states from lawsuits brought forth by out-of-state citizens or foreigners.

Twelfth Amendment

The Twelfth Amendment was ratified in 1804. It established that the president and vice president would be elected as a team by an electoral college. Previously, the president and vice president had been elected separately. The candidate with the most electoral votes became president, and the person with the next-highest number of electoral votes became vice president.

Thirteenth Amendment

The Thirteenth Amendment, ratified in 1865, is one of the most important in United States history. It abolished slavery and involuntarily being a servant, except when being a servant is punishment for a crime.

Fourteenth Amendment

The Fourteenth Amendment, ratified in 1868, defined citizenship more clearly and contains the very important Equal Protection Clause. It defines citizens as "all persons born or naturalized in the United States." In other words, every United States citizen is protected under U.S. laws.

The Equal Protection Clause is cited in many civil rights cases to this day. It has been used in numerous court cases involving discrimination against people from various groups. One such notable case was 1954's *Brown v. Board of Education*, which ended racial segregation in schools in the United States. It was also the basis for the Supreme Court ruling that same-sex couples be guaranteed the right to legally marry. The Fourteenth Amendment also removed the designation of slaves as counting as three-fifths of a person in the Constitution.

Fifteenth Amendment

The Fifteenth Amendment, ratified in 1870, prohibited states from denying certain citizens the right to vote based on race, color, or previous servitude. In a sense, this was a political move. Republican president Ulysses S. Grant had been elected to office partly because he had support from black male voters. The Republican Party wanted to capitalize on this popularity, so it was in their best interests to allow minorities and former slaves to vote.

Sixteenth Amendment

The Sixteenth Amendment was ratified in 1913. It gave Congress the right to levy a tax that was not based on the U.S. census population.

Suffragettes fought valiantly to secure voting rights for women.

Seventeenth Amendment

Also ratified in 1913, the Seventeenth Amendment changed how senators are elected. Previously, they were appointed by state legislators. But under the Seventeenth Amendment, they are now elected by direct popular vote.

Eighteenth Amendment

The Eighteenth Amendment, ratified in 1919, prohibited the manufacturing and sale of alcohol in the United States.

This amendment was ratified in January 1919, but **repealed** in 1933. The amendment was not successful. People found ways to make and sell alcohol, even though it was illegal.

Nineteenth Amendment

In 1920, the Nineteenth Amendment was ratified. It gave women the right to vote, and prohibited states from denying people the right to vote based on gender.

Twentieth Amendment

The Twentieth Amendment, was ratified in 1933. It changed the dates on which the presidential and vice presidential terms would begin, as well as the terms for senators and representatives.

Twenty-First Amendment

The Twenty-First Amendment, also ratified in 1933, repealed the Eighteenth Amendment, but made it a federal offense to transport or import (bring in to sell) alcohol into states where importing alcohol was illegal.

Twenty-Second Amendment

The Twenty-Second Amendment limited presidential terms. Ratified in 1951, it states that a person can be elected president only twice. If that person has taken the presidency with more than two years left in the term, such as when a vice president replaces a president who died in office, that person can be elected president only one more term.

Twenty-Third Amendment

The Twenty-Third Amendment, which was ratified in 1961, gave Washington, D.C., electors in the electoral college.

Twenty-Fourth Amendment

The Twenty-Fourth Amendment, ratified in 1964, was yet another amendment addressing voting rights. It established that no state could revoke a citizen's voting rights if that citizen could not pay a poll tax or other related tax. This was largely in response to the Southern states establishing poll taxes designed to deny black citizens and poor citizens the right to vote. The Southern states did not want black citizens to vote because it might change the white-dominated political structure in the South. However, the Fifteenth Amendment prohibited them from denying black citizens the right to vote.

A number of amendments address citizens' rights to vote in the United States.

So instead, Southern states created taxes they knew most black citizens could not afford to pay. In that way, they denied black citizens and other poor citizens the right to vote. The Twenty-Fourth Amendment outlawed that practice.

Twenty-Fifth Amendment

Ratified in 1967, the Twenty-Fifth Amendment established presidential succession in the event of an incapacitated or deceased president. It also established procedures for filling a vice presidential vacancy if the vice president had to step into the position of president.

Twenty-Sixth Amendment

The Twenty-Sixth Amendment, ratified in 1971, is yet one more amendment addressing voting rights. It granted citizens the right to vote at the age of 18. This amendment came about during the Vietnam War era. At that time, citizens pointed out that it was unfair that young people were deemed adult enough to go off to war at age 18, but not considered adult enough to vote.

Twenty-Seventh Amendment

The Twenty-Seventh Amendment, ratified in 1992, has the distinction of being the amendment with the longest ratification timespan. It was introduced in 1789, but not ratified for almost 203 years. It delays laws affecting congressional salaries from taking effect until after the next election cycle. In other words, pay raises for members of Congress cannot take effect until after the next election.

HOW WELL DO YOU UNDERSTAND AMERICAN DEMOCRACY?

If you were a member of Congress, what other amendments to the Constitution would you propose?

CHAPTER 5

A Living Document

The Constitution can be interpreted in two ways. The first is a literal interpretation of how the Framers wrote it. The second is as a "living document," which relies on the spirit of the law, and updates the interpretation based on modern society. The Supreme Court and the federal court system often rely on constitutional law to make important decisions, so how the document is interpreted is important.

The Literal Interpretation

A literal interpretation, or most basic explanation, of the Constitution is often known as a historical interpretation, or as interpreting its original purpose. In this interpretation, courts look to historical documents and the writings of the Framers to interpret their intent, or purpose. For example, *The Federalist Papers* is an often-cited, or quoted, source when interpreting the Constitution in this way, and so are the notes from the Constitutional Convention.

Historical literalists interpret the document by looking only at the words written in the Constitution to form their **opinion**. They also consider what the words meant when the document was written, since the meanings of words can change over time. They do not look at outside sources from the time. Their assessment is based solely on the words of the Constitution. Contemporary, or modern-day, literalists do the same thing as historical literalists, except they do not consider a change in the meaning of words over time. They form their interpretation based only on the words in the Constitution and what the meanings of those words are today.

In the Supreme Court, some justices view the Constitution as a living document, while others interpret it as the Framers intended it when they wrote it.

The Living-Document Interpretation

Another method of interpreting the Constitution involves seeing it as a living document. That is, a document whose interpretation changes over time, based on the changes in society. The spirit of the document remains intact, but the interpretation may change as times change. This is sometimes called a modernist interpretation.

Courts using a living-document interpretation feel that applying laws written more than 200 years ago to current cases is unrealistic without acknowledging that times have changed from when the document was written.

One often-used example is in regard to gun laws. When James Madison wrote the Second Amendment (see page 26), the main weapons in use were muskets, single-shot cannons, flintlock pistols, and other similar weapons. They could certainly kill a person, but they could not likely be used to kill many people at a time. Today, semiautomatic and assault weapons are available that can fire multiple rounds within seconds.

The AR-15 assault rifle, which is widely available in the United States, has been used in a number of mass shootings in recent years. It can be modified to hold up to 100 rounds of ammunition, which can be fired as fast as the shooter can pull the trigger. The shooter in the tragedy at Sandy Hook Elementary School, for example, killed 26 people, mostly children, in a matter of moments using that model of gun. Glocks, which can be purchased after a three-day waiting period, can hold 15 rounds of ammunition and fire rapidly.

Those who view the Constitution as a living document argue that Madison did not wish to arm citizens with weapons capable of killing large numbers of people in a very short period of time. Madison wrote about the "right to bear arms" in the context of muskets and flintlock pistols. This, they argue must be taken into account with interpreting the Constitution.

This memorial was created to honor those who lost their lives in the Sandy Hook Elementary School shooting. Many people cite mass shootings such as this as a reason for stricter gun-control measures.

MARRIAGE EQUALITY AND THE LIVING CONSTITUTION

One relatively recent landmark Supreme Court decision was the 2015 ruling in favor of marriage equality. This ruling made it illegal for states to refuse to issue marriage licenses to same-sex couples or to refuse to recognize the validity of same-sex marriages.

The 5-to-4 Supreme Court ruling in June 2015 was the source of much debate. The Constitution itself does not mention marriage—and thus, it does not define it as being between a man and a woman or being between any two adults. As it is not mentioned in the Constitution, many feel that it is up to each state to determine whether to recognize same-sex marriage.

However, supporters of same-sex marriage argue the Equal Protection Clause in the Fourteenth Amendment covers this issue when it says that no state shall "deprive any person of life, liberty, or property, without due process of law; nor deny to any person within its jurisdiction the equal protection of the laws." Marriage, they say, is a liberty, and the Fourteenth Amendment clearly states that no person shall be deprived of a liberty.

Justice Anthony Kennedy, who wrote the Supreme Court decision on same-sex marriage, supports the idea of a living Constitution. He commented that the people who wrote the Fourteenth Amendment could not presume to know all of the dimensions of freedom that would occur as the years passed. He noted that, therefore, the rights protected in the Fourteenth Amendment would expand and change as society evolved.

It is worth noting that the justices who opposed the majority ruling were not necessarily against gay rights. Rather, they simply believed that the Constitution did not mention marriage, and so marriage—whether heterosexual or same-sex—was not an issue that should be decided by federal law. They argued that it was overstepping the Constitution to make marriage a federal issue.

Also, those who favor a living-document interpretation argue that parts of the Constitution were deliberately written with vague, or nonspecific, language to allow it to be a living document that would change as the nation grew. For example, the Constitution specifically does not mention the words "slave" or "slavery" because the Framers were not sure the institution of slavery would be permanent. So, they left the document deliberately vague. People who favor viewing the Constitution as a living document point to vague sections like this as proof that the Constitution was meant to be a flexible document that would update as morals and beliefs of society changed.

Those who view the Constitution as a living document also point to more than 200 years of case law as setting legal precedent, which is a new rule established in a previous case. In reviewing legal precedent for two centuries, the meaning of the Constitution naturally shifts as each new decision becomes part of history.

Justice Ruth Bader Ginsburg interprets the Constitution as a living document.

A Happy Medium

In deciding cases, no judge who must interpret and apply constitutional law always uses only a literal or only a living-document interpretation of the Constitution. Judges generally combine tactics and form an interpretation that is based on the intent of the Framers of the Constitution, and the fact that times have changed, so some flexibility in interpretation is needed. However, many judges lean a bit more toward one type.

For example, Supreme Court Justice Ruth Bader Ginsburg is known for leaning toward a living-document interpretation of the Constitution. However, her former fellow justice, the now-deceased Antonin Scalia, often favored a more literal interpretation. Justice Clarence Thomas also tends to favor a more literal interpretation.

This is part of why it is essential to have a varied panel of judges in the Supreme Court. That way, each judge can weigh in with their interpretation, and as a collective court, they debate their positions and write an opinion on a case. This means the ultimate opinion is based on the literal interpretation of the Constitution, by legal precedent from earlier cases and by interpretation of a living Constitution. The hope is that this means the best, most accurate judgment in any given case.

The pro-life vs. pro-choice debate rages on, despite the Supreme Court ruling years ago in favor of a woman's right to choose.

HOW WELL DO YOU UNDERSTAND AMERICAN DEMOCRACY?

Abortion rights have also been a hotly debated topic in the court system. Pro-life groups have longed to overturn *Roe v. Wade* since the Supreme Court's 1973 landmark decision. How might a literal interpretation of the Constitution support or not support a woman's right to choose? What about a living-document interpretation?

CHAPTER 6

The Supreme Court

The Constitution is the law of the land in the United States and is an incredibly important part of Supreme Court rulings. The Supreme Court uses the Constitution when determining cases that then inform rulings in lower courts. In addition to *Brown v. Board of Education* and *Roe v. Wade*, there have been many other landmark cases that have used the Constitution as a basis for Supreme Court decisions that have changed the face of the United States legal system.

A Case Against Affirmative Action

Minority citizens had long faced a double standard in the United States. They could perform at a job or in school as well as a white citizen, yet the white citizen got better treatment. Perhaps that was higher pay, or perhaps it was admittance to a university. The situation played out many times in many ways, and the end result was nearly always the same: white citizens had more rights than minorities, despite what the law said. As a result, affirmative action worked to correct those injustices.

In the academic setting, this meant improved access to education for people from underprivileged and minority groups. Some universities established quotas for the number of students from a particular ethnic group that should be accepted in a given year. Some argued that this could lead to a situation where a white student was denied admission so that a minority student could be given a place at a university.

Allan Bakke argued this in the *Regents of the University of California v. Bakke* case. Bakke was a 35-year-old white man who had twice applied to the medical school program at the University of California at Davis. Despite having good grades and high test scores, Bakke was denied admission. He later learned that minority applicants with lower test scores and lower grade-point averages had been admitted to the medical school while he was denied. These students fell into the university's specialty admissions program.

Bakke filed a lawsuit, saying that he was denied admission to the medical school based on his race. He stated that this was a clear violation of the Equal Protection Clause in the Fourteenth Amendment. In 1978, the Supreme Court ruled in Bakke's favor, finding that the university had indeed violated constitutional law.

It is an unusual case because historically in the U.S., white men have not been victims of racial discrimination. However, other Supreme Court cases based on the Equal Protection Clause have ruled in favor of men as the subject of gender bias, which is also surprising. Historically, women have been the victims of gender bias, not men. But the Supreme Court is fairly adamant in its rulings that the Equal Protection Clause applies to all citizens.

Affirmative action has helped students of color access higher education across the U.S.

A Case Against Self-Incrimination

In 1963 in Arizona, a man named Ernesto Miranda was arrested for kidnapping and raping a 17-year-old girl. He was taken to the police station to take part in a lineup, after which the officers on the case suggested that he had been positively identified by the victim. Miranda then confessed to the officers, who had not informed him of the Fifth Amendment right protecting him from self-incrimination, or the Sixth Amendment right that he was entitled to an attorney's assistance. The Fifth Amendment states, "[No person] shall be compelled in any criminal case to be a witness against himself," and the Sixth Amendment states, "the accused shall…have the Assistance of Counsel for his defence."

The United States Constitution is the ultimate law of the land. Justices of the Supreme Court look to the Constitution to make their rulings.

Miranda was found guilty of kidnapping and assault, mainly because of his confession. However, because the officers failed to inform Miranda of his rights under these two amendments, he was able to appeal the court's decision. The Arizona Supreme Court upheld the lower court's ruling, but Miranda appealed to the Supreme Court, which ruled in his favor and overturned his original conviction.

The state of Arizona later chose to retry Miranda without his confession admitted as evidence. He was again convicted of kidnapping and rape. However, the Supreme Court's ruling brought about a change in law enforcement that exists to this day. All persons being arrested must be read the Miranda warning—those famous lines that start, "You have the right to remain silent."

The Legacy of the Constitution

While constitutional law is not an exact science, and how it is applied depends on how the Constitution is interpreted by any given judge, the fact is that the Constitution is the law of the land in the United States. When all efforts to decide a legal case have failed to bring about a decision, the Supreme Court looks to the Constitution as a basis for its decisions.

The Constitution may not be flawless but it provides a framework under which a strong nation can operate and govern. At times, the language in the document is vague, but that vagueness allows room for a more flexible interpretation. In a nation where society's values and beliefs are always evolving, the flexibility is necessary.

In years to come, the Constitution will continue to be the basis of the United States legal system. As the United States continues to embrace individuals from various nationalities and ethnic backgrounds, the Constitution will continue to be the document that binds the society in which all these citizens live.

The Constitution in Action

November 15, 1777	Articles of Confederation adopted by Continental Congress
March 1, 1781	Articles of Confederation ratified by all 13 states
September 17, 1787	United States Constitution created
June 21, 1788	United States Constitution ratified
March 4, 1789	United States Constitution takes effect
September 25, 1789	Bill of Rights created
December 15, 1791	Bill of Rights ratified

Glossary

abolition The process of doing away with something.

autonomy Freedom from external influence.

bicameral Consisting of two branches or chambers.

checks and balances A system that balances power in a government, ensuring that all power is not left in the hands of one individual or a small group.

Committee of the Whole A legislative strategy in which all members sit as part of a single committee.

double jeopardy The prosecution of the same person twice for the same offense.

due process Fair treatment through the U.S. judicial system.

electoral college The body of official voters, representing each state, who formally cast the votes for the president of the United States.

federalism A system of government that divides power between a national government and state governments.

Framers of the Constitution The delegates who went to the Constitutional Convention and drafted the Constitution.

indentured servants People who signed contracts requiring them to work for several years in exchange for gaining passage to the U.S.

indictment A written statement formally charging a person with a serious crime.

opinion In law, a formal statement of reasons supporting a given judgment.

popular vote A simple form of election in which the candidate with the most votes wins.

precedents In law, previous cases or decisions that are followed in similar later cases.

quorum A minimum number of members that must be present at a meeting to make the meeting proceedings official.

ratified Given formal consent to a new law, treaty, contract, or agreement, thus making it official.

repealed Cancelled.

self-incrimination The act of exposing oneself or confessing either directly or indirectly.

separation of powers The principle that power is divided among three branches of government: the executive, legislative, and judicial.

sovereign states States with borders and governments that make laws the citizens of that state follow.

unicameral Made up of a single chamber or branch.

For More Information

Books

Grafton, John (ed.). *The Declaration of Independence and Other Great Documents of American History 1775–1865*. Mineola, NY: Dover Thrift Editions, 2000.

Hamilton, Alexander, James Madison, and John Jay. *The Federalist Papers*. London: Arcturus Publishing Limited, 2016.

Skousen, Paul B. *How to Read the Constitution and the Declaration of Independence*. Salt Lake City, UT: Izzard Ink, 2017.

Vile, John R. *The United States Constitution: One Document, Many Choices*. London: Palgrave Macmillan, 2015.

Websites

This National Archives page contains links to other important historical documents, including the Declaration of Independence and the Bill of Rights:
www.archives.gov/founding-docs/constitution-transcript

This website provides the full text of the Constitution and its amendments:
www.constituteproject.org/constitution/United_States_of_America_1992

The Library of Congress website is an excellent source of primary documents that are crucial pieces of American history:
www.loc.gov/rr/program/bib/ourdocs/Constitution.html

The White House website provides the full text of the Constitution, as well as helpful historical background information:
www.whitehouse.gov/1600/constitution

Publisher's note to educators and parents: Our editors have carefully reviewed these websites to ensure that they are suitable for students. Many websites change frequently, however, and we cannot guarantee that a site's future contents will continue to meet our high standards of quality and educational value. Be advised that students should be closely supervised whenever they access the Internet.

Index